Contents

2 Huge homophones

4 *a* or *an*?

6 Wild word families

8 *ch* words

10 *y* or *i*?

12 *ou* words

14 Apostrophes

16 Discovering dictionaries

18 More apostrophes

20 Word endings

22 Punctuation

24 Prefixes

26 Tiny tenses

28 When and why

30 *le*, *el*, *il* and *al* endings

32 More tenses

34 Perfect plurals

36 Suffixes

38 Adding information

40 Checking your work

42 Quick test

44 Explorer's logbook

46 Answers

Introduction

If you are wild about learning and wild about animals – this book is for you!

It will take you on a wild adventure, where you will practise key English skills and explore the amazing world of big and small animals along the way.

Each English topic is introduced in a clear and simple way with lots of interesting activities to complete so that you can practise what you have learned.

Alongside every English topic you will uncover fascinating facts about the world's largest and smallest animals.

When you have completed each topic, record the animals that you have seen and the skills that you have learned in the explorer's logbook on pages 44–45.

Good luck, explorer!

Alison Head

Huge homophones

FACT FILE

Animal: Blue whale
Habitat: Almost all the world's oceans
Weight: Up to 180 000 kg
Lifespan: 80 to 90 years
Diet: Small crustaceans called krill

Words that **sound the same** but have **different meanings and spellings** are called **homophones**. They can be easy to mix up so we have to be careful to use the correct word. Look at these examples:

whale   *wail*

Task 1   Circle the correct word to complete each sentence.

a Whales spend most of <u>there/their/they're</u> lives swimming alone.

b I hoped to see a whale but I could not find <u>won/one</u>.

c Whales can <u>here/hear</u> each other up to 1600 km away.

d The whale was <u>two/too/to</u> far away for me to see clearly.

e Whales do have <u>hare/hair</u> but only a very small amount.

f Whales use their <u>tails/tales</u> to slap the water.

Task 2

Write a homophone for each of these words.

a due _____

b groan _____

c son _____

d great _____

e pair _____

f bear _____

Task 3

Write a sentence using each of these words.

a sea _____

b see _____

c for _____

d four _____

e where _____

f wear _____

Exploring Further ...

Unscramble these pairs of homophones.

a lera _____ eler _____

b frloo _____ lwaf _____

c igrht _____ ewitr _____

d lueb _____ lwbe _____

e neba _____ ebne _____

Now swim to pages 44–45 to record what you have learned in your explorer's logbook.

3

a or an?

When you write about one thing, you often need to use **a** or **an** first.

a is used before words that start with a **consonant** sound:

a hummingbird

an is used before words that start with a **vowel** (a, e, i, o, u) sound:

an explorer

FACT FILE

Animal: Bee hummingbird

Habitat: Forests and woodland on the island of Cuba

Weight: 1.95 to 2.6 g

Lifespan: Up to 7 years

Diet: Nectar

WILD FACT

The bee hummingbird is the world's smallest bird. The female lays two 6 mm eggs in a tiny cup-shaped nest made with cobwebs and lichen.

Task 1 **Complete each sentence with *a* or *an*.**

a The hummingbird hovered by _____ flower.

b The explorer made _____ exciting discovery.

c Travellers should be well-prepared before setting out on _____ journey.

d _____ bee hummingbird is a truly tiny animal.

e The bee hummingbird is only as big as _____ bumble bee.

f The male bee hummingbird has _____ amazing red-pink head.

Task 2   Is **a** or **an** used correctly in each sentence? Put ✓ or ✗ in the boxes.

a I read an chapter in this book about bee hummingbirds. ☐

b A explorer photographed the bee hummingbird's nest. ☐

c Bee hummingbirds beat their wings 80 times a second. ☐

d A bee hummingbird can fly for up to 20 hours without landing. ☐

e The bee hummingbird is an amazing creature! ☐

f I can't believe it is a real bird! ☐

Task 3   Write five words which could follow *a* and five that could follow *an*.

a a _____   an _____

b a _____   an _____

c a _____   an _____

d a _____   an _____

e a _____   an _____

WILD FACT

Bee hummingbirds eat half their body mass in nectar each day.

Exploring Further ...

Think of a word to complete each sentence and write it in the space.

a I read an _____ book about bee hummingbirds.

b The bee hummingbird is a _____ animal.

c It would be wonderful to travel to a _____.

d The photograph clearly showed an _____.

e The glossy feathers make a _____ picture.

Now fly to pages 44–45 to record what you have learned in your explorer's logbook.

Wild word families

FACT FILE

Animal: African bush elephant

Habitat: The savannah, deserts and rainforests of Africa

Weight: Up to 10 000 kg

Lifespan: Up to 70 years

Diet: Roots, grasses, fruit and bark

Task 1 Sort these words into families. Write each family in a leaf.

unsafe reapply familiarity saviour apply application unfamiliar safest familiarise

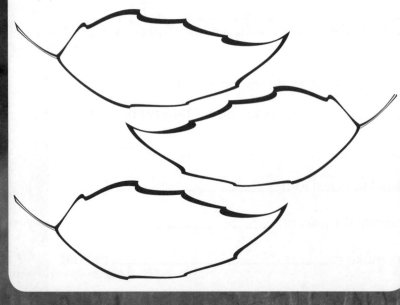

Task 2

Add two words that would belong to the same family as each of the words shown.

a contain _____ _____

b regret _____ _____

c allow _____ _____

d follow _____ _____

WILD FACT

These elephants live in complex societies guided by the oldest female animal, called the matriarch. She decides when the group rests, bathes and drinks.

Task 3

Work out these words. They are all from the same family. Some letters have been given to help you.

a football p l _ _ _ r

b school p _ _ y _ _ _ _ _ d

c _ l _ y f _ _ puppy

d _ _ a _ i _ g tennis

WILD FACT

African bush elephants are the largest land-dwelling mammals and the second tallest after the giraffe.

Exploring Further ...

Find these words in the word-search grid.

V	A	L	A	V	U	E	D	L
D	L	L	E	A	L	N	E	D
B	E	V	A	L	U	A	T	E
S	U	A	S	U	V	A	E	U
V	A	L	U	A	B	L	E	L
T	T	U	W	T	B	I	D	A
L	U	E	E	I	C	L	M	V
O	E	R	T	O	T	I	E	L
Y	D	L	M	N	L	L	V	E

value

valuable

valuation

evaluate

valued

Now charge to pages 44–45 to record what you have learned in your explorer's logbook.

7

ch words

Meet the Chihuahua. It is a lovely little dog but its name is difficult to read and to spell!

The letters **ch** can make **different sounds**, even in easier words. Try reading these words out loud:

school   chips   chef

Getting to know words like this will make them easier to read and spell.

Task 1   Find and copy two words from the box in which the **ch** sound matches these words.

mechanic   chill   chandelier   brochure   echo   charm

a chair   _____   _____

b monarch   _____   _____

c chalet   _____   _____

Task 2   Colour the correctly spelt word in each pair of bones.

a stomack   stomach

b shampoo   champoo

c chaos   caos

d technical   tecknical

e machine   mashine

f shivalry   chivalry

| **Task 3** | Write a sentence using these words. |

a choir _____

_____

b chauffeur _____

_____

c which _____

_____

d scheme _____

_____

e chip _____

_____

f charge _____

_____

Exploring Further ...

Add the missing letters to complete these words. Use the picture clues to help you.

a   a _ c _ _ _ r

b   m _ _ _ s t _ _ _ e

c    c _ _ _ _ _

d   p _ _ a _ h _ _ _ _

Now run to pages 44–45 to record what you have learned in your explorer's logbook.

y or i?

WILD FACT

The caterpillars of the western pygmy butterfly provide ants with a nectar liquid in return for protection. Sounds like a fair deal!

Some words which sound like they are spelt with an **i** actually contain a **y**, like this creature's name: *western pygmy blue butterfly*

We need to learn these words and remember how to spell them.

Task 1   Add **y** or **i** to complete these words.

a   m __ stery

b   h __ story

c   rh __ thm

d   r __ ddle

e   hab __ t

f   prett __ ly

Task 2   Circle the correctly spelt word in each pair of caterpillars.

a   myth   mith

b   symbol   simbol

c   wryggle   wriggle

d   optimyst   optimist

e   typical   tipycal

f   critical   crytical

Task 3 — Draw a line from each word to its meaning.

a cymbals   beats in a word

b anonymous   round metal musical instrument

c syrup   of unknown name

d syllable   Australian animal

e platypus   thick, sticky sugary liquid

FACT FILE

Animal: Western pygmy blue butterfly

Habitat: Across southern USA and Central America

Weight: Almost nothing!

Lifespan: Adult butterflies live for around a week

Diet: Nectar

Exploring Further ...

Find these words in the word-search grid.

E	D	N	O	E	L	E	A
D	K	L	O	G	A	M	P
S	O	N	E	I	P	C	H
S	Y	M	P	H	O	N	Y
X	L	S	K	O	A	L	S
O	N	Y	T	X	D	J	I
W	O	P	S	E	N	O	C
A	L	Y	D	I	M	Y	A
A	M	L	E	A	Y	A	L

symphony

physical

system

onyx

lynx

Now flutter to pages 44–45 to record what you have learned in your explorer's logbook.

ou words

FACT FILE

Animal: African goliath frog
Habitat: The rainforests of western Africa
Weight: More than 3 kg
Lifespan: Up to 15 years
Diet: Insects, small fish and amphibians

The letters **ou** can make the same sound as **u** in some words.

Read this word out loud:

enough

WILD FACT

At up to 32 cm in length, African goliath frogs are as big as some pet cats!

Task 1 Add **u** or **ou** to complete each word.

a disc___rage

b n___rish

c b___rrow

d b___nting

e t___gh

f wr___ng

g h___ng

h sp___rt

Task 2 Underline a mistake in each sentence. Write the correct word on the line.

a Explorers show currage in exploring new places. _____

b I saw a cupple of goliath frogs hopping along. _____

c African goliath frog tadpoles flurrish in fast streams. _____

d The explorer went to a lot of trubble to find the frog. _____

e He travelled over rugh territory searching for it. _____

Task 3   Add the missing letters to complete a word that rhymes with each of these words.

a   much   t _ _ _ _

b   rubble   d _ _ _ _ _

c   tongue   y _ _ _ _

d   cuff   r _ _ _ _

Task 4   These words have the letters **ou** missing from them. Write the words again, with **ou** in the right place.

a   jeals   _____

b   fams   _____

c   hazards   _____

d   fabuls   _____

e   nervs   _____

f   varis   _____

g   obvis   _____

h   curis   _____

WILD FACT

Despite being the world's biggest frog, the tadpoles of African goliath frogs are the same size as tadpoles of ordinary frogs.

Exploring Further ...

Write one sentence using all three of these words.

country   encourage   youngest

_____

_____

Now hop to pages 44–45 to record what you have learned in your explorer's logbook.

Apostrophes

Apostrophes do an important job. They can be used to show that something belongs to someone or something.

If you are writing about **one person or thing**, the apostrophe goes before the **s**, like this:

A horse's hooves

If you are writing about more than one person or thing, the apostrophe usually goes after the **s**, like this:

Two horses' hooves

Some plurals do not end in **s**. With these words, the apostrophe goes before the **s**, like this:

The men's saddles

FACT FILE

Animal:	Falabella miniature horse
Habitat:	Originally bred on the plains of Argentina
Weight:	18 to 45 kg
Lifespan:	Up to 30 years
Diet:	Grass and hay

Task 1   Add an apostrophe to each phrase.

a   an explorers notebook

b   the suns warmth

c   two scientists discoveries

d   three horses tails

e   all of the ladies hats

f   a mares food

g   a grey ponys mane

h   two childrens hats

WILD FACT

The Falabella is the smallest breed of horse. All Falabellas originally came from the Falabella farm in Argentina.

Turn the singular nouns into their plurals.

Singular	Plural
horse's ear	
man's hat	
child's toy	
baby's rattle	
woman's book	
person's vote	
trainer's foot	

WILD FACT

Falabellas are easily trained. They are sometimes used to help people with disabilities, just like guide dogs.

Task 3 Is the apostrophe in the correct place in these sentences? Tick yes or no for each one.

a Peoples' love of Fallabellas means they are famous across the world.
  yes ☐ no ☐

b A Fallabellas' tiny hoof prints could be seen at the edge of the forest.
  yes ☐ no ☐

c This books' illustrations shows Fallabellas of many different colours.
  yes ☐ no ☐

d An explorers' aim is to explore animal habitats.
  yes ☐ no ☐

e The trainer's goal was to teach her Fallabella to pull the cart.
  yes ☐ no ☐

Exploring Further ...

Write TRUE or FALSE next to each statement.

a With a singular noun, the apostrophe always goes before the s. _____

b With plural nouns, the apostrophe always goes after the s. _____

c With words like *people* and *children*, the apostrophe goes before the s. _____

Now trot to pages 44–45 to record what you have learned in your explorer's logbook.

Discovering dictionaries

Dictionaries can tell you how to **spell** words and **what they mean**. The words in a dictionary are arranged in **alphabetical order** to help you find the word you need.

Look at these words:

jellyfish   jumper   junk

If two words start with the same letters, they are arranged according to the second or third letters.

FACT FILE

Animal: Lion's mane jellyfish
Habitat: Arctic, northern Atlantic and northern Pacific Oceans
Weight: More than 1000 kg
Lifespan: Up to 1 year
Diet: Plankton, small fish and jellyfish

Task 1   Write these words again in alphabetical order.

a beetle   bear   bell   creak   break   crate

_____

b jump   keep   joy   jelly   kick   jay

_____

Task 2

Write down one word you would find between each pair of words in the dictionary.

a dance _____ frog   **b** light _____ link

c train _____ trap   **d** swamp _____ swim

e chase _____ cinema   **f** leaflet _____ lemon

Task 3

Use a dictionary to check the spelling of these words.
Write a definition for each word.

a restaurant _____

b relative _____

c ridiculous _____

d reduce _____

e revolve _____

f return _____

WILD FACT

Like all jellyfish, the mouth of the lion's mane jellyfish is found underneath its bell-shaped body.

WILD FACT

The world's largest jellyfish, the lion's mane jellyfish, is poisonous and can create its own light.

Exploring Further ...

Number the books one to five to put them in alphabetical order on the shelf.

Explorer's Handbook ☐
Discovering Wildlife ☐
Creatures of the Sea ☐
Exciting Animals ☐
Diary of an Explorer ☐

Now float to pages 44–45 to record what you have learned in your explorer's logbook.

More apostrophes

Apostrophes are used when **letters are taken out** to join two words together in a contracted form, like this:

was not   wasn't

The **apostrophe replaces the letter or letters** that have been removed.

Task 1

Draw lines to match up the pairs of words with the correct contracted form.

a do not   I'm

b she is   we're

c we are   we won't

d he will   don't

e I am   she's

f we will not   he'll

WILD FACT

Speckled padloper tortoises have five toes on their front feet.

Task 2

Write down the contracted form for each of these phrases.

a should not   _____

b they are   _____

c will not   _____

d are not   _____

e we would   _____

f you are   _____

Task 3 Write down the letter or letters that each apostrophe has replaced.

a she'll _____

b they'd _____

c can't _____

d it's _____

e they're _____

f it'll _____

WILD FACT

The speckled padloper tortoise is the world's smallest tortoise. It is less than 11 cm in length.

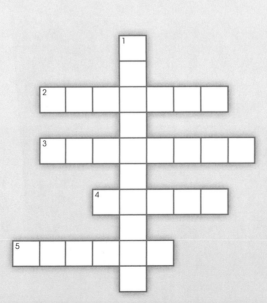

Exploring Further ...

Find the full form of these contracted words in the crossword grid.

Across
2. it'd
3. couldn't
4. I've
5. we've

Down
1. should've

Now crawl to pages 44–45 to record what you have learned in your explorer's logbook.

Word endings

The word endings **sion**, **ssion**, **cian** and **tion** all sound very similar. Try reading these words out loud:

expansion   profession   mathematician   rejection

We need to learn which ending to use. You will discover that **tion** is the most common ending.

Task 1

Add the correct ending to each word. Use the clues to help you.

a man _____ (a big house)

b pa _____ (strong feelings)

c opti _____ (fits spectacles)

d electri _____ (fixes wiring)

e pen _____ (income in old age)

f permis _____ (allowing something)

FACT FILE

Animal:	Giant barrel sponge
Habitat:	Caribbean Sea, Bahamas, Barbados and the reefs around Florida
Weight:	Up to 80 kg
Lifespan:	Up to 2000 years!
Diet:	Bacteria, viruses and tiny particles of plants

Task 2 Colour the correctly spelt word in each pair of shells.

a mician | mission

b confecian | confession

c tension | tencian

d musician | musision

e politission | politician

f extension | extencian

WILD FACT

Giant barrel sponges are extremely primitive. They don't have proper organs, like a heart or brain.

Task 3 Write a sentence using these words.

a action _____

_____

b discussion _____

_____

c comprehension _____

_____

d magician _____

_____

Exploring Further ...

Unscramble these words. Some letters have been given to help you.

a VEINTOINN   I _ _ _ _ _ _T _ _ _ _

b SISODAMIN   _ D M _ _ _ S _ _ _ _

c ATRONI   R A _ _ I _ _ _

Now waft to pages 44–45 to record what you have learned in your explorer's logbook.

Punctuation

Punctuation marks help our readers to understand our writing.

Full stops, **question marks** and **exclamation marks** at the end of a sentence tell us what kind of sentence it is.

Commas separate items in a list or show you where to pause when reading.

Inverted commas go before and after **direct speech**, to show that someone is speaking.

FACT FILE

Animal:	Pygmy marmoset
Habitat:	Forests of Brazil, Peru, Colombia and Ecuador
Weight:	100 g
Lifespan:	10 to 12 years
Diet:	Tree sap, fruit, nectar, leaves and insects

WILD FACT

The lower teeth of pygmy marmosets are adapted to carve holes in the bark of trees to get at the sap, gum or resin underneath.

Task 1 Add a full stop, question mark or exclamation mark to these sentences.

a A pygmy marmoset is about 15 cm long

b Have you ever seen a pygmy marmoset

c Those monkeys are totally amazing

d Have you discovered where marmosets live

e A pygmy marmoset is the world's smallest monkey

Task 2   Add the missing commas to these sentences.

a   The pygmy marmoset feasted on sap leaves and berries.

b   The explorer packed water food a map and a compass for the journey.

c   You find out about wildlife from zoos libraries and websites.

d   Pygmy marmosets are found in Brazil Peru Colombia and Ecuador.

e   The pygmy marmoset is prey for cats eagles hawks and snakes.

Task 3   Add the missing inverted commas to these sentences.

a   There's a marmoset in that tree!'
    exclaimed the explorer.

b   I managed to take a photograph of
    it,' replied the wildlife photographer.

c   The explorer commented, 'That will
    look great in our logbook.

d   'I'll see if I can take another one,
    added the photographer.

e   'I can count nine marmosets in that
    tree! said John.

WILD FACT

The pygmy marmoset is the world's smallest monkey. They are only active during the day, huddling together in the trees at night to keep warm.

Exploring Further ...

Add the missing punctuation to this passage.

The explorers trekked into the forest They saw colourful birds tiny frogs and large snakes Look up there shouted their guide Can you see the marmosets in the trees

Now leap to pages 44-45 to record what you have learned in your explorer's logbook.

Prefixes

Prefixes are letters that you can add to the start of some words to **alter their meaning.** Some prefixes allow us to turn words into their **antonyms**. These are words that are opposite in meaning.

Here are some examples:

agree	→	disagree
behave	→	misbehave
active	→	inactive
legible	→	illegible
perfect	→	imperfect
regular	→	irregular

Task 1 Choose one of the prefixes in the eggs to turn each word into its antonym. Write the word you have made in the space.

(mis) (ir) (im) (il) (un) (dis)

a mature _____

b logical _____

c inform _____

d responsible _____

e obey _____

Task 2

Add a prefix to each word to make its antonym.

a edible _____

b replaceable _____

c agree _____

d correct _____

e legal _____

f perfect _____

Ostriches defend themselves from predators by kicking with their strong legs. Each foot has a long, sharp claw that can kill a lion.

Task 3

Join the bubbles to make four words.

resistible   ir   dis

understand   appear

patient

mis

im

Exploring Further ...

Find the antonyms of these words in the word-search grid

D	M	M	D	I	S	L	O	M	R
E	I	M	M	O	R	A	L	I	O
S	R	S	I	M	M	T	A	L	D
H	O	T	H	I	N	F	S	T	E
M	P	H	I	O	L	T	S	T	Y
I	M	I	S	I	N	F	O	R	M
S	N	A	N	T	I	E	A	T	E
I	I	L	O	A	T	E	S	S	E
I	L	L	I	T	E	R	A	T	E
I	N	A	B	I	L	I	T	Y	L

honest

moral

inform

literate

ability

Now sprint to pages 44–45 to record what you have learned in your explorer's logbook.

Tiny tenses

FACT FILE

Animal: Barbados threadsnake
Habitat: Forests on the island of Barbados
Weight: 0.6 g
Lifespan: Unknown
Diet: Insect larvae

Tenses tell us whether something is happening **now**, happened in the **past** or will happen in the **future**, like this:

| I explore | I explored | I will explore |

When you write, you must make sure that you are using the right tense all the way through.

Task 1 Complete the table by filling in the past tense verbs. The first one has been done for you.

Present tense	Past tense
walk	walked
search	
bring	
wake	
live	
sleep	

WILD FACT

Barbados threadsnakes were only discovered in 2008, so scientists do not know very much about them yet.

WILD FACT

The Barbados threadsnake is thought to be the world's smallest snake. It is just over 10 cm in length and thinner than a strand of spaghetti.

Task 2 Write these sentences again, correcting the tense of the bold verb.

a Yesterday the explorer **finds** a Barbados threadsnake under a rock.

_____

b The snake **is** tiny and it looked like a scrap of grey string.

_____

c The explorer **takes** a photograph of the snake.

_____

d He **lets** the snake go free after he measured it.

_____

Task 3 Write these sentences again in the present tense.

a The explorers were finding out about the wildlife on Barbados.

_____

b I was hoping they would be able to find the tiny eggs of the Barbados threadsnake.

_____

_____

c Scientists were discovering more about them every day.

_____

Exploring Further ...

Decide whether each sentence is written in the past tense, present tense or future tense. Write **past**, **present** or **future** on the line.

a Barbados snakes were discovered quite recently. _____

b I will be researching them for my project next week. _____

c These snakes are only found in one small patch of forest. _____

Now slither to pages 44–45 to record what you have learned in your explorer's logbook.

When and why

When we are writing, special words can help us to describe when and why something has happened.

when   because   then   soon   before   during

Task 1 Add these words to the table in the correct box.

because   so   while   after   before   therefore   then   later

Words describing *when* something happened	Words describing *why* something happened

Choose the most suitable bold word in the brackets to complete each sentence.

a The spider scuttled across the cave wall _____ sprang at its prey. (**soon next then**)

b Giant huntsman spiders move quickly _____ they are hard to catch. (**because so then**)

c _____ we were watching the spider, it caught a large insect. (**So During While**)

d It will _____ be time for the explorers to go back to their base camp. (**soon then next**)

e People are often afraid of giant huntsman spiders _____ they are so large. (**therefore so because**)

Task 3 Write an appropriate ending for each of these sentences.

a There was thunder and lightning so _____

b During the evening, _____

c We were late back because _____

d The explorers set off into the jungle but soon _____

WILD FACT
Look out! These huge spiders move very quickly with a crab-like motion.

Exploring Further ...

Unscramble these **when** and **why** words.

a SEEBCAU _____

b FREOHTEER _____

c GURDNI _____

d HLIWE _____

Now scuttle to pages 44–45 to record what you have learned in your explorer's logbook.

le, el, il and al endings

Task 1 Colour the correctly spelt word on each pair of honey pots.

a (tabel)   (table)

b (metal)   (metle)

c (lable)   (label)

d (fossle)   (fossil)

e (rebal)   (rebel)

f (stable)   (stabel)

The word endings **le**, **el**, **il** and **al** all sound very similar. Say these words out loud:

battle   tunnel   lentil   pedal

This can make these words tricky to spell. You need to learn which words have each ending.

FACT FILE

Animal: Sun bear
Habitat: Rainforests of Southeast Asia
Weight: Up to 70 g
Lifespan: Up to 25 years
Diet: Fruit, insects, small animals and honey

Task 2 Write **el**, **al**, **il** or **le** to complete each word.

a squirr _____   d tow _____

b capit _____   e bott _____

c nostr _____   f nibb _____

Task 3 Underline the mistake in each sentence. Write the correct word on the line.

a Explorers traval to faraway places to find out about animals.

_____

b The explorer tracked the animel into the trees.

_____

c In the middel of the forest, the sun bear climbed a tree.

_____

d A littal bear cub was curled up in the branches.

_____

e The wind rocked the branches like a cradel.

_____

WILD FACT

Sun bears are also known as honey bears. They have a really long tongue, so they can get honey out of bees' nests.

WILD FACT

Sun bears are the world's smallest bear. Despite their name, sun bears are nocturnal. They sleep in the branches of the trees all day.

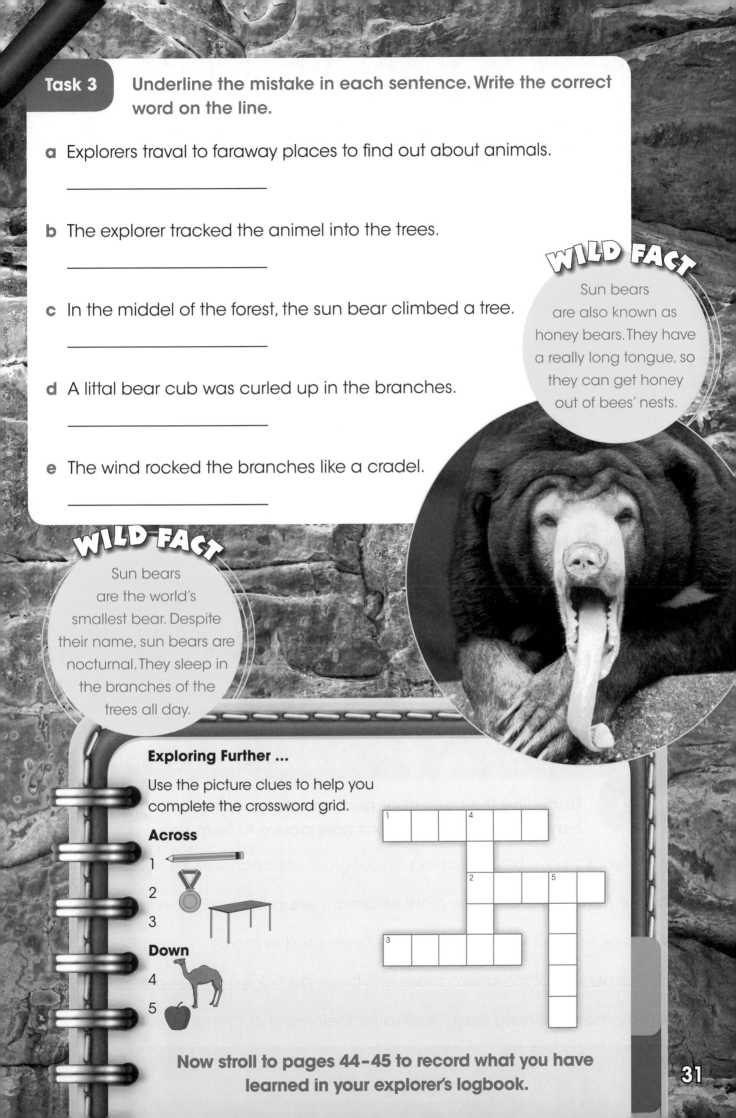

Exploring Further ...

Use the picture clues to help you complete the crossword grid.

Across

1

2

3

Down

4

5

Now stroll to pages 44–45 to record what you have learned in your explorer's logbook.

Tenses are a way to change verbs to help us describe when something is done. If we are writing about something that happened in the past and is finished, we use the simple past.

The salamander <u>rested</u> at the edge of the river.

If we are writing about something that started in the past but still carries on, we use the present perfect tense.

The salamander <u>has rested</u> at the edge of the river for hours.

WILD FACT

The world's largest amphibian, the Chinese giant salamander, grows up to 1.8 metres in length, but their tadpoles are just 3 cm long.

Task 1   Underline the present perfect verb form in these sentences. Look at the example above to help you.

a Scientists have been learning about giant salamanders for years.

b The numbers of Chinese giant salamanders in the wild have fallen.

c Chinese giant salamanders have been bred in zoos.

d The habitat of the salamander has been damaged by people.

e Salamanders have been hunted for their meat in China.

Tick the sentence that includes the present perfect verb tense.

a The giant salamander hid in the murky water. ☐

b The explorer photographed a Chinese giant salamander. ☐

c Relatives of the salamander have lived on earth for millions
of years. ☐

Task 3 Write these sentences again, replacing the verb in **bold**
with the present perfect tense.

a People **hunted** these salamanders for food.

_____

b Scientists **discovered** that the stream was polluted.

_____

c The pollution **killed** the Chinese giant salamanders.

_____

WILD FACT

Chinese giant salamanders make a wailing noise which sounds so like a crying human child that they are known as 'infant fish' in Chinese.

Exploring Further ...

Find the simple past forms of these present perfect verbs in the word-search grid. The first one has been found for you.

has written

has seen

has known

has run

has left

has woken

W	L	A	E	K	W
A	R	A	N	J	E
S	S	O	A	E	K
L	E	A	T	L	O
R	K	K	N	E	W
U	N	E	C	F	K
N	E	S	W	T	Q

**Now swim to pages 44–45 to record what you have
learned in your explorer's logbook.**

Perfect plurals

Plurals allow us to write about more than one thing but there are spelling rules you need to know.

To turn most nouns into a plural, you just add **s**:

animal ⟶ animals

If the noun ends in **s**, **sh**, **x**, **zz**, or **ch**, you add **es**:

bush ⟶ bushes

For words ending in a consonant followed by **y**, remove the y and add **ies**:

baby ⟶ babies

With words ending in **f**, you usually remove the f and add **ves**:

wolf ⟶ wolves

Some words change completely when they are plural:

mouse ⟶ mice

Some words do not change at all!

sheep ⟶ sheep

Task 1

Write the plural of each of these nouns.

a explorer _____

b fox _____

c wish _____

d pebble _____

e lady _____

f monkey _____

Task 2 Circle the correct plural in each pair.

a shelf: shelfs shelves

b pony: ponies ponys

c deer: deers deer

d man: men mans

e life: lifes lives

f foot: feet foots

Task 3 Sort these words into the table depending on how you turn them into plurals.

poppy witch loaf leaf party forest discovery half glass creature key bus

add s	add es	remove the y and add ies	remove the f and add ves

Exploring Further ...

Unscramble these plural nouns then draw lines to match them with the correct singular noun.

a NHRLICDE _____ goose

b TTEHE _____ louse

c LEOPPE _____ tooth

d EEGES _____ child

e ELCI _____ person

Now scurry to pages 44–45 to record what you have learned in your explorer's logbook.

Suffixes

Suffixes are letters or **groups of letters** we can add to the **end of some words** to change their meaning.

Words with more than one syllable that end with a consonant are tricky.

Take care when you add a suffix beginning with a vowel.

If the final syllable of the word is stressed when you say it, you often need to double the final consonant before adding the suffix:

forget   forgetting

If the final syllable is not stressed, you can just add the suffix:

garden   gardener

FACT FILE

Animal: Atlas moth
Habitat: Tropical and subtropical dry forests of Southeast Asia
Weight: 25 g
Lifespan: As adults, 1 to 2 weeks
Diet: Adult Atlas moths do not eat

WILD FACT

Adult Atlas moths have no mouths when they emerge from their cocoons. They never eat but rely on fat stored from when they were caterpillars.

Task 1

Complete these word sums, doubling the final consonant of the root word where necessary.

a regret + ing = _____

b pedal + ed = _____

c widen + ed = _____

d refer + ing = _____

e metal + ic = _____

f transfer + ed = _____

Circle the correctly spelt word in each pair.

a marvellous marvelous   b rivaled rivalled

c sharpener sharpenner   d modeling modelling

e labelling labeling   f shriveled shrivelled

Task 3 Choose a suitable word from the box to complete each sentence.

| different   traveller   limited   labelled   preference |

a The _____ spent months on a ship.

b The scientist _____ her specimens carefully.

c The explorers' investigation was _____ by the terrible weather.

d I have a _____ for finding out about moths and butterflies.

e There were many _____ moths and butterflies in the forest.

WILD FACT

Atlas moths are thought to be named after the patterns on their huge wings, which look like maps.

Exploring Further ...

Find these words hidden in the word-search grid.

limitation   beginner

offering   developing

regretting

R	B	E	A	L	D	O	L	E	D
D	E	V	E	L	O	P	I	N	G
E	G	G	L	L	E	D	M	O	O
D	I	E	R	J	O	P	I	P	F
E	N	T	D	E	L	E	T	E	F
A	N	H	R	T	T	A	A	D	E
L	E	S	I	T	R	T	T	R	R
E	R	I	A	A	L	D	I	E	I
R	G	H	S	E	I	V	O	N	N
G	B	E	G	I	E	N	N	U	G

Now flit to pages 44–45 to record what you have learned in your explorer's logbook.

Adding information

Expanded noun phrases allow us to **add information to nouns**. They help us to make our writing more interesting.

We can use **adjectives** to add information:

the tiny chameleon

We can also add extra nouns and adjectives:

the chameleon with the curled tail

WILD FACT

The minute leaf chameleon is among the smallest chameleons, measuring less than 4 cm in length.

FACT FILE

Animal:	Minute leaf chameleon
Habitat:	Forests of Madagascar
Size:	Up to 3.3 cm
Lifespan:	Unknown
Diet:	Tiny flies

Task 2
Draw a line to join the beginning of the sentence to a sensible ending.

a He was a curious explorer   with thousands of tall trees.

b He saw a tiny movement   because of the rain.

c It was a tiny chameleon   with an interest in reptiles.

d The forest was crowded   amongst the fallen leaves.

e We could not see anything   which was completely unknown to scientists.

Add a suitable adjective from the box to complete each sentence.

> strong   active   larger   smaller   small

a The chameleons were discovered in a _____ area of forest.

b They are _____ during the day but hide in the trees at night.

c It is possible that even _____ chameleons exist.

d Many _____ chameleons have the ability to change their skin colour.

e Minute leaf chameleons can use their _____ tails for stability.

WILD FACT

Unlike their larger cousins, minute leaf chameleons cannot change the colour of their skin.

Exploring Further ...

Think about the animals you have read about in this book. Draw lines to join up the two halves of these expanded noun phrases in the most sensible way.

a	the large, rare	lion's mane jellyfish
b	the small, thread-like	African pygmy mouse
c	a tiny, fast-moving	Chihuahua
d	the small, shivering	Chinese giant salamander
e	the huge, poisonous	Barbados thread snake

Now crawl to pages 44–45 to record what you have learned in your explorer's logbook.

Checking your work

When you have finished writing, you should always leave time to read through your work carefully to **look for mistakes** you have made. This is called **proofreading**.

Check your **spelling** and **punctuation** and make sure your **sentences all make sense**.

FACT FILE

Animal: Flemish giant rabbit
Habitat: Kept as a companion animal across the world
Weight: 7 to 8 kg
Lifespan: Up to 5 years
Diet: Hay, grass and small amounts of leafy vegetables

Task 1   Underline the spelling mistakes in these sentences. Write the correct word on the line.

a   We went too the petting zoo to see the giant rabbits.   _____

b   A labal on their cage told us they like to eat hay.   _____

c   I wanted to buy won but they need a lot of space.   _____

d   There were donkies at the zoo too.   _____

e   There paddock was next to the piglets.   _____

Task 2   Add the missing punctuation to these sentences.

a Have you ever seen a Flemish giant rabbit

b 'They are bigger than my cat! said Katie.

c That rabbits ears are enormous!

d Id love to have a pet rabbit.

e Their fur is very soft

WILD FACT

The Flemish giant is the world's biggest breed of rabbit. Originally bred for their meat and fur, now they make popular pets.

Task 3   Write these sentences again, correcting the mistakes.

a The rabbites we sore were really big.

_____

b One was licking it's pores and washing its face.

_____

c Would you like to feed them an treat asked they're keeper?

_____

WILD FACT

Flemish giants can be trained to recognise their names and can make good house pets if trained from a young age.

Exploring Further ...

Write TRUE or FALSE next to each of these sentences.

a Apostrophes replace the letters that are removed when two words are joined together.   _____

b 'There' is the word you use when you want to write that something belongs to 'them'.   _____

c Inverted commas go at the start and end of direct speech.   _____

d The plural of 'leaf' is 'leaves'.   _____

Now hop to pages 44–45 to record what you have learned in your explorer's logbook.

Quick test

Now try these questions. Give yourself 1 mark for every correct answer – but only if you answer each part of the question correctly!

1 **Write down a homophone for this word.**
road _____

2 **Underline the correct bold word to complete the sentence.**
The explorer made a (**amazing fascinating**) discovery.

3 **Which root word is found in each of these words?**
signature design signage signpost _____

4 **Underline the word where ch makes a hard k sound.**
chute chemical

5 **Underline the correctly spelt word.**
pigmy pygmy

6 **These words all contain the letters ou. Read them out loud, then circle the one where ou sounds different from the others.**
scout mouth cousin mountain

7 **Add the possessive apostrophe to this sentence.**
The mens water bottles were empty.

8 **Write these words again in alphabetical order.**
packet patch parchment pacing

_____ _____ _____ _____

9 **Write the correct contracted form of this phrase.**
they have _____

10 **Add c, ss, t or s to complete this word.**
compa _____ ion

11 **Add the missing inverted commas to this sentence.**
This animal is tiny! exclaimed the explorer.

12 **Is this sentence written in the past tense, present tense or future tense?**
I love finding out about animals. _____

13 **Which of the prefixes in the box could be added to all of these words?**

| ir il in im |

active complete sufficient

_____ _____ _____

42

14 **Underline the word that helps you understand when the explorer found the butterfly.**

After reaching the top of the mountain, the explorer saw the butterfly.

15 **Circle the incorrectly spelt word in this group.**

cradle   stabel   noble   cable

16 **Write this sentence again, using the present perfect.**
Scientists discovered a new animal.

_____

17 **Write down the plurals for these words:**

patch   _____

cry   _____

half   _____

18 **Circle the correctly spelt word in this pair.**
happenning   happening

19 **Add a suitable adjective to complete this sentence.**

It was a _____ journey through the forest.

20 **Underline two mistakes in this sentence.**

The explorer packed a emergency pack four the journey.

Write the sentence correctly.

_____

_____

How did you do?   1–5 Try again!   6–10 Good try!
11–15 Great work!   16–20 Excellent exploring!

/20

43

Explorer's Logbook

Tick off the topics as you complete them and then colour in the star.

How do you feel?
- Needs practice
- Nearly there
- Got it!

Apostrophes ☐

Huge homophones ☐

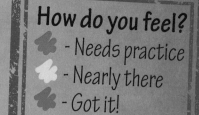
ch words ☐

y or i? ☐

a or an? ☐

More apostrophes ☐

ou words ☐

Wild word families ☐

Discovering dictionaries ☐

Punctuation ☐

Adding information ☐

le, el, il and al endings ☐

Word endings ☐

Suffixes ☐

When and why ☐

Perfect plurals ☐

Prefixes ☐

Tiny tenses ☐

Checking your work ☐

More tenses ☐

Answers

Pages 2–3

Task 1

a their   **b** one   **c** hear

d too   **e** hair   **f** tails

Task 2

a dew   **b** grown   **c** sun

d grate   **e** pear or pare   **f** bare

Task 3

Any sentence is acceptable that is grammatically correct and uses the given word in an appropriate context.

Exploring Further

a real, reel   **b** floor, flaw   **c** right, write

d blue, blew   **e** bean, been

Pages 4–5

Task 1

a a   **b** an   **c** a

d A   **e** a   **f** an

Task 2

Correct answers: **c, d, e, f**

Task 3

Any words starting with a consonant are acceptable to follow **a**.

Any words starting with a vowel are acceptable to follow **an**.

Exploring Further

Any words are acceptable which are appropriate in that context and start with a vowel or consonant as required.

Pages 6–7

Task 1

unsafe, saviour, safest

reapply, apply, application

familiarity, unfamiliar, familiarise

Task 2

Possible answers include:

a container, contained, containing

b regrettable, regretful

c allowed, allowance, allowable

d following, follower, followed

Task 3

a football player   **b** school playground

c playful puppy   **d** playing tennis

Exploring Further

V	A	L	A	V	U	E	D	L
D	L	L	E	A	L	N	E	D
B	E	V	A	L	U	A	T	E
S	U	A	S	U	V	A	E	U
V	A	L	U	A	B	L	E	L
T	T	U	W	T	B	I	D	A
L	U	E	E	I	C	L	M	V
O	E	R	T	O	T	I	E	L
Y	D	L	M	N	L	L	V	E

Pages 8–9

Task 1

a chair, chill, charm

b monarch, mechanic, echo

c chalet, chandelier, brochure

Task 2

a stomach   **b** shampoo   **c** chaos

d technical   **e** machine   **f** chivalry

Task 3

Any sentences are acceptable which are grammatically correct and use the given word in an appropriate context.

Exploring Further

a anchor   **b** moustache

c chain   **d** parachute

Pages 10–11

Task 1

a mystery   **b** history   **c** rhythm

d riddle   **e** habit   **f** prettily

Task 2

a myth   **b** symbol   **c** wriggle

d optimist   **e** typical   **f** critical

Task 3

a cymbals – round metal musical instrument

b anonymous – of unknown name

c syrup – thick, sticky sugary liquid

d syllable – beats in a word

e platypus – Australian animal

Exploring Further

E	D	N	O	E	L	E	A
D	K	L	O	G	A	M	P
S	O	N	E	I	P	C	H
S	Y	M	P	H	O	N	Y
X	L	S	K	O	A	L	S
O	N	Y	T	X	D	J	I
W	O	P	S	E	N	O	C
A	L	Y	D	I	M	Y	A
A	M	L	E	A	Y	A	L

Pages 12–13

Task 1

a discourage   **b** nourish   **c** burrow

d bunting   **e** tough   **f** wrung

g hung   **h** spurt

Task 2

a currage – courage   **b** cupple – couple

c flurrish – flourish   **d** trubble – trouble

e rugh – rough

Task 3

a touch   **b** double

c young   **d** rough

Task 4

a jealous   **b** famous   **c** hazardous

d fabulous   **e** nervous   **f** various
g obvious   **h** curious

Exploring Further
Any sentence is acceptable which is grammatically correct and uses the given words in an appropriate context.

Pages 14–15
Task 1
a explorer's   **b** sun's
c scientists'   **d** horses'
e ladies'   **f** mare's
g pony's   **h** children's

Task 2

Singular	Plural
horse's ear	horses' ears
man's hat	men's hats
child's toy	children's toys
baby's rattle	babies' rattles
woman's book	women's books
person's vote	people's votes
trainer's foot	trainers' feet

Task 3
a No   People's
b No   Fallabella's
c No   book's
d No   explorer's
e Yes   trainer's

Exploring Further
a TRUE   **b** FALSE   **c** TRUE

Pages 16–17
Task 1
a bear, beetle, bell, break, crate, creak
b jay, jelly, joy, jump, keep, kick

Task 2
Any words are acceptable which could be found between the two given words in a dictionary.

Task 3
a a business where food is prepared and served to customers
b a person from the same family
c silly, foolish or absurd
d make smaller
e turn around and around
f go back to where you were

Exploring Further
5. Explorer's Handbook   3. Discovering Wildlife
1. Creatures of the Sea   4. Exciting Animals
2. Diary of an Explorer

Pages 18–19
Task 1
a do not – don't   **b** she is – she's
c we are – we're   **d** he will – he'll
e I am – I'm   **f** we will not – we won't

Task 2
a shouldn't   **b** they're   **c** won't
d aren't   **e** we'd   **f** you're

Task 3
a she'll: w i   **b** they'd: w o u l **or** h a
c can't: n o   **d** it's: i **or** h a
e they're: a   **f** it'll: w i

Exploring Further
Across: 2. it would 3. could not 4. I have 5. we have
Down: 1. should have

Pages 20–21
Task 1
a mansion   **b** passion   **c** optician
d electrician   **e** pension   **f** permission

Task 2
a mission   **b** confession   **c** tension
d musician   **e** politician   **f** extension

Task 3
Any sentence is acceptable which is grammatically correct and uses the given word in an appropriate context.

Exploring Further
a INVENTION   **b** ADMISSION   **c** RATION

Pages 22–23
Task 1
a A pygmy marmoset is about 15 cm long.
b Have you ever seen a pygmy marmoset?
c Those monkeys are totally amazing!
d Have you discovered where marmosets live?
e A pygmy marmoset is the world's smallest monkey.

Task 2
a The pygmy marmoset feasted on sap, leaves and berries.
b The explorer packed water, food, a map and a compass for the journey.
c You find out about wildlife from zoos, libraries and websites.
d Pygmy marmosets are found in Brazil, Peru, Colombia and Ecuador.
e The pygmy marmoset is prey for cats, eagles, hawks and snakes.

Task 3
a 'There's a marmoset in that tree!' exclaimed the explorer.
b 'I managed to take a photograph of it,' replied the wildlife photographer.
c The explorer commented, 'That will look great in our logbook.'
d 'I'll see if I can take another one,' added the photographer.
e 'I can count nine marmosets in that tree!' said John.

Exploring Further

The explorers trekked into the forest. They saw colourful birds, tiny frogs and large snakes. 'Look up there!' shouted their guide. 'Can you see the marmosets in the trees?'

Pages 24–25

Task 1

a immature   **b** illogical   **c** misinform

d irresponsible   **e** disobey

Task 2

a inedible   **b** irreplaceable   **c** disagree

d incorrect   **e** illegal   **f** imperfect

Task 3

impatient, misunderstand, irresistible, disappear

Exploring Further

D	M	M	D	I	S	L	O	M	R	
E	I	M	M	O	R	A	L	I	O	
S	R	S	I	M	M	T	A	L	D	
H	O	T	H	I	N	F	S	T	E	
M	P	H	I	O	L	T	S	T	Y	
I	M	I	S	I	N	F	O	R	M	
S	N	A	N	T	I	E	A	T	E	
I	I	L	O	A	T	E	S	S	E	
I	L	L	I	T	E	R	A	T	E	
I	N	A	B	I	L	I	T	Y	L	

Pages 26–27

Task 1

walk – walked   search – searched

bring – brought   wake – woke

live – lived   sleep – slept

Task 2

a found   **b** was   **c** took   **d** let

Task 3

a The explorers are finding out about the wildlife on Barbados.

b I am hoping they are able to find the tiny eggs of the Barbados threadsnake.

c Scientists are discovering more about them every day.

Exploring Further

a past   **b** future   **c** present

Pages 28–29

Task 1

When: while, after, before, then, later

Why: because, so, therefore

Task 2

a then   **b** so   **c** While

d soon   **e** because

Task 3

Any appropriate ending is acceptable which completes a sentence which is grammatically correct.

Exploring Further

a BECAUSE   **b** THEREFORE

c DURING   **d** WHILE

Pages 30–31

Task 1

a table   **b** metal   **c** label

d fossil   **e** rebel   **f** stable

Task 2

a squirrel   **b** capital   **c** nostril

d towel   **e** bottle   **f** nibble

Task 3

a traval – travel   **b** animel – animal

c middel – middle   **d** littal – little

e cradel – cradle

Exploring Further

Across: 1. pencil 2. medal 3. table

Down: 4. camel 5. apple

Pages 32–33

Task 1

a have been learning   **b** have fallen

c have been bred   **d** has been damaged

e have been hunted

Task 2

c

Task 3

a have hunted   **b** have discovered

c has killed

Exploring Further

W	L	A	E	K	W
A	R	A	N	J	E
S	S	O	A	E	K
L	E	A	T	L	O
R	K	K	N	E	W
U	N	E	C	F	K
N	E	S	W	T	Q

Pages 34–35

Task 1

a explorers   **b** foxes   **c** wishes

d pebbles   **e** ladies   **f** monkeys

Task 2

a shelves   **b** ponies   **c** deer

d men   **e** lives   **f** feet

Task 3

add s	add es	remove the y and add ies	remove the f and add ves
forest	witch	poppy	loaf
creature	bus	party	leaf
key	glass	discovery	half

Exploring Further

a CHILDREN – child   **b** TEETH – tooth

c PEOPLE – person   **d** GEESE – goose

e LICE – louse

Pages 36–37

Task 1

a regretting   **b** pedalled   **c** widened

d referring   **e** metallic   **f** transferred

Task 2

a marvellous   **b** rivalled   **c** sharpener

d modelling   **e** labelling   **f** shrivelled

Task 3

a traveller   **b** labelled   **c** limited

d preference   **e** different